How to Write the Perfect Cover Letter – in less than 30 Minutes

A guide for online and offline job applications

Jack Staff

Copyright © 2017 Jack Staff

All rights reserved.

ISBN: 9781520232447

TO L, H AND J.

In memory of JMP.

CONTENTS

1	Introduction	1
2	The mechanics	3
3	The letter	7
4	A word about your language	19
5	Sample cover letter	25
6	About the author	27

1 – INTRODUCTION

Many people spend hours agonising over their cover letter. But they never find out if it was worth the effort. Others barely give it a moment's thought, then wonder why they get such a poor response.

The purpose of this book is to tell you everything you need to know about the vexed cover letter. It will show you how to write it effectively for any job you care to apply for. It will explain the standards that recruiters expect.

By the time you've finished this book, you'll know everything you ever need to know. You'll be able to dash off an excellent, tailored cover letter in about half an hour.

WHAT ARE COVER LETTERS FOR?

Your cover letter has one job, and one job only – to get a recruiter to read your curriculum vitae (CV) or résumé. The instant the recruiter moves onto your CV, or onto the next application, it's done, finished, spent, dead.

Your cover letter is used to screen you. It's the first thing a recruiter uses to make a yes or no decision. In short, the cover letter sends your application into the "read and consider" pile, or into the confidential shredding.

In a cover letter, recruiters are looking for:

- Tailored skills that match the job description
- Clarity – the job applied for, well written, easy to read format
- Especially pertinent details from your CV
- Reasons why they should hire you as a person
- A well-presented document
- Brevity!

The purpose of this book is show you how to write the sort of cover letter recruiters are looking for – every time.

2 – THE MECHANICS

It's important to get the basics right. If you really know what you're doing, and the jobs you apply for call for high levels of impact management, you can aim to make a bigger splash. But if you're simply applying for regular jobs, either by post or online, it's easier and probably more effective to use the conventional tools in the usual way.

ON PAPER

Print your cover letter onto plain, white copying paper. It should be standard 80gsm to 90gsm paper, the same material you print your CV on.

The paper should be the same size as your CV, which should be standard business paper size – A4 around most of the world, or letter size in the USA.

If you want to use personal, pre-printed stationery, fine, but make sure it's white, cream or a light, neutral tone. Avoid pastel shades unless you're applying for a position in a nursery. The point is to make your application as readable as humanly possible. That means your ink colour should be black. Avoid the temptation to "stand out" by using dark or mid tones of blue or grey. Yes, your application will stand out, but not in a good way.

LENGTH

Every recruiter has individual preferences, so you need to aim for the least annoying. That means one side, including addresses and salutations. Aim for half a page of content, around 200 to 250 words. Getting a word count is simple in most word processing programs. Just highlight the body of your letter, click the word count feature.

If you go on any longer than a couple of hundred words, you'll be reproducing your CV. Don't do that.

LAYOUT

Make sure your leave margins of about 3 cm to 3.5 cm (about an inch and a half) top, bottom, left and right. It should be the page setup default settings on your word processing software.

Unless you're hoping to impress with your design skills, keep the font simple. It must be easy to read. You should be aware that fonts with a serif are a little easier to read on paper, while one without serifs is better on screen. If you want to pick a one-size-fits-all font, choose something plain without serif like Arial or Calibri. Avoid cursive and decorative scripts.

The font size must be readable. In Arial, 10 pt is the minimum you should use – 10.5 pt is better. But 11 pt and 12 pt start to look like clown shoes. In order to make Arial readable, your line spacing needs to be a nudge bigger than single. If you format line spacing at

1.5 lines, that's the upper limit. Your letter will look nice and airy, but you won't have a lot of room for content.

So, if you're using 10 pt Arial, have a look at setting the line spacing to "exactly" 13 pt or 14 pt. If you want to use Arial 11 pt, aim for "exactly" 14 pt or 15 pt. Check how the line spacing affects the overall length of your cover letter. Remember – one side, maximum.

Calibri is a tighter font, so you'd need to use 11.5 pt or 12 pt for basic legibility. But the line spacing is better, so you can probably just use single spacing, rather than the slightly expanded layout that Arial needs.

Experiment a little and see what looks best to you. Whether you plan to send a hard copy or not, print out your cover letter (the same advice applies to your CV, too) and see how readable it is. Even if you email your documents, and most people do these days, there's a fair chance the recruiter may want to print your application out. If it's not easy to read, your application won't get the attention it deserves.

EMAIL

When you email an application, don't force the recruiter to open up a separate cover letter in order to see who they are dealing with. Include your cover letter in the main body of the email, and attach your CV.

Unless you're instructed otherwise, in the subject line include the job reference, for example:

Subject: *Application for IT Manager – reference ITM/123/2016*

Send your email as plain text, so it can be read by any email reader. Yes, you lose some of your exquisite formatting, but unless you're trying to impress visually, it's all grist to the mill. Besides, there's a good chance your application will be machine-read, and machines are notoriously unfussy about elegant presentation.

The comments about length and layout on paper do apply equally to emailed letters. There's a chance the recruiter might want to print out your cover letter as well as your CV, so it has to be as readable as a hard copy letter sent in the mail.

3 – THE LETTER

If you only achieve one thing with your cover letter, it must be customised. That is, you must tailor your letter to the specific job you're applying for. Match your skills with the requirements set out in the job specification, and your application will be read. A candidate that matches the job specification is precisely what the recruiter is looking for.

If your cover letter screams: "This candidate is a great fit!", your CV gets read. At that point, your CV needs to persuade the recruiter that you're worth talking to or meeting. But your cover letter sells your CV and your CV sells you.

Yes, tailoring every letter might sound like hard work if you intend to send off dozens of applications. But each cover letter shouldn't take you more than half an hour, when you get the hang of it.

MAN VERSUS MACHINE?

If you apply for jobs online, the chances are that your application will be "read" by software. This saves the cost of paying real people.

Now, people are infinitely smarter than any programme ever devised at reading a CV, interpreting what it says, and making a spot-on call. But once job applications made the transition to largely online activity at the click of a mouse button, the number of candidates went through the roof. The lack of effort needed meant people could blitz the internet with applications in the hope that something might stick.

So, many applications are from complete no-hopers. Consequently, recruitment consultants have harnessed the stamina (if not the intelligence) of computers to carry out the application sifting and to identify candidates that meet the employer's criteria.

In order to convince the machines that your application meets the job requirements, the essence of your cover letter is to parrot back the skills sought by the job specification.

PREAMBLE

At the top, make sure your name, mailing address, email and telephone number are clear. In some parts of the world it is customary to align right these lines. In others, you can centre them.

The name and address of the recruiter (or organisation) is usually aligned left and comes next.

Don't forget to include the date somewhere.

SALUTATION

If you possibly can, use the recruiter's name. It's a warm touch and helps you visualise a real human instead of a stone-faced gatekeeper blocking the path to your dreams.

Where no name is mentioned in the job advertisement, it's easy to call a company's switchboard, say you're applying for a job, and ask who should you address it to.

In general, you should echo the style the recruiter uses. But if your application is the first contact, then err on the side of formal.

It's always better to begin:

> *Dear Mr Smith,*
>
> *Dear Ms Brown,*

Use the title (Mr, Ms, Mrs, Miss, Lord, Bishop, etc.) used in the recruitment advertisement. For women, *Ms* is the generally accepted form if no other preferred title is given.

If no named contact is given, it's safe to assume that the recruiter doesn't care much. As it seems rude to put nothing, how about one of these?

> *Dear Recruiter,*
>
> *Dear Sir or Madam,*
>
> *Dear HR Team,*
>
> *Dear Shackleton & Sons (Plumbers) Ltd,*

Or even:

> *To whom it may concern (okay, this is the comedy option.)*

Emails are less formal, but if you wish, write the same salutation you would for a letter: *Dear Mr Smith, Dear Ms Brown*, etc. Again, echo the style of the recruiter. If you've been in touch – for example to ask about some aspect of the position – then if they reply…

> *Dear Cuthbert,*

> *Hi, Jemma!*

…copy their style in return.

Generally, though, you can use first names in emails, but keep it semi-formal by using "Dear" rather than "Hi!" unless you know for sure the recruiter uses that degree of informality.

JOB REFERENCE

Either above or below the salutation, include the job reference if there is one. The reason is obvious. There's no point putting together a magnificent application for a job as a soccer coach if the recruiter is left thinking: "But she's got no experience at all as a dinner lady!"

Make it easy to read – centre and bold.

Application for IT Manager – reference ITM/123/2016

Whether it's read by a human or a box, if they mistake

the job you want, you'll never get it.

LETTER CONTENT

The perfect cover letter consists of four paragraphs. Each paragraph has a particular role. You only have half a side at most to sell your CV, so get straight to the point. It's not being brusque – you're saving the recruiter time plodding through dozens of self-indulgent personal stories.

FIRST PARAGRAPH – APPLY FOR THE JOB

Your opening paragraph should be short and to the point and explain why it is that you're writing. Ignore any temptation to fly off into the realms of the florid.

State quite simply that you're applying for a job / position / role / appointment, and say what that job is. If you saw the job advertised in a journal or website, it's good manners to let the recruiter know which medium worked. If it was a personal recommendation, a hat tip to that person is both courteous and a tacit endorsement. That's it.

Examples:

> *I would like to apply for the position as Head of Marketing which was advertised on gudjobs.com.*

> *I would like to be considered for the job of Transport Supervisor, which one of your drivers, John Smith, mentioned was becoming available.*
>
> *I saw your advertisement in the Daily Scrounger for a Vehicle Fitter. I would like to apply for that job.*

The recruiter only gleans two pieces of information in the second he or she spends reading that paragraph – the position you want and the source of your information. All other information is unnecessary.

SECOND PARAGRAPH – WHY YOU ARE SUITABLE FOR THE JOB

This is the place where you say you are a good fit for the position you're applying for. Go through the job advertisement and list (in order of priority) the job skills the position is asking for. If the position was shown on a website, the chances are there are half a dozen bullet points listing the requirements for the job. If you're applying for the job, you must meet these criteria.

Very quickly establish your academic and professional qualifications for the job – one sentence can do this.

Examples:

> *I have a degree in mathematics and am a qualified chartered accountant.*

> *I have an HND in engineering and am a full member of the Institute of Mechanical Engineers.*
>
> *I am a qualified solicitor with a particular interest in business and contract law.*
>
> *I have a PSV licence and ten years experience driving buses and coaches.*

Then, go through each of the main requirements of the job and explain how you meet the top three to five. You won't have room in a cover letter for more. But your CV should demonstrate that you meet all the mandatory requirements and many of the "desirable" ones too.

If your application is going to be read by computer software, it's best to repeat the exact language describing the requirements that the job specification uses. That's what software is programmed to look out for and match with. The recruitment jargon may grate, but it's the line of least resistance.

How do you know if it's a non-human? If you apply online and use an online application form, that's likely to be scanned by a machine before a human sees it. Look at the numbers who have applied. If it's dozens, expect a machine to do the first sift. Otherwise, avoid jargon as far as possible. Describe how you meet the job specification in natural terms.

Some examples of addressing job requirements in a cover letter:

Job requirement	Your cover letter
Significant experience of driving financial accounting systems and process change with demonstrable achievements	*I spent three years implementing a new Snodgrass Accounting information System, refreshing all the procedures, retraining staff, eliminating the need for temporary staff and interim managers.*
Cleaning a large kitchen area in a four star hotel, washing pots and pans by hand	*I have four years experience hand washing both pots and crockery in a primary school kitchen and in a country pub at weekends.*
Previous experience as a people leader in a call centre environment or similar – Essential	*I have run customer teams in three call centres.*
You will also have strong involvement in sport as a player, coach or volunteer.	*I am a former professional rugby player, currently volunteering as a coach for a colts' team.*
A working knowledge of cell culturing.	*I have two years experience in continuous cell lines and regulating physico-chemical environments.*

THIRD PARAGRAPH – WHAT YOU CAN DO FOR THEM

Beyond the strict requirements of the position, what can you uniquely offer the potential employer? The third paragraph is where you sketch out very briefly the sorts of things that you personally embody. These are personal skills, aptitudes and qualities. You can't simply assert that you have characteristic X or Y; you show, don't tell. Explain, very briefly, how you have the personal skills you present. What demonstrates these qualities?

Examples of communication, team working, problem solving and leadership skills are especially desirable to all employers. Depending on the job, attention to detail and persistence might be important. It might be useful to show you can handle unexpected problems. You might have complementary creative skills to the main business.

Examples:

> *In addition to the job requirements, I am an experienced and confident presenter and public speaker, which I feel is important in a communications business.*
>
> *I have a particular interest in helping disabled employees and am proficient in British Sign Language.*
>
> *As a volunteer fire-fighter, I am used to dealing with unexpected, dangerous problems.*

> *I understand screen printing and have written a number of articles published in trade magazines.*
>
> *I enjoy the world of design and am an accomplished amateur photographer.*
>
> *As a former insurance assessor, I am used to working with people in emotional distress.*
>
> *I am sure-handed and accomplished at dealing with the public firmly and politely, with ten years experience as a part-time bouncer.*
>
> *With five years experience in refuse collection, I am an effective supervisor, trainer and safety officer.*
>
> *I should also mention that I am a qualified First-Aid provider.*
>
> *I would like to emphasise my language skills, as I speak fluent German and conversational Danish.*

Almost every previous job gives you some experience that is valuable to a future employer. Even if your only previous job is a paper round, you can say in your cover letter:

> *Unusually for a graduate, I am happy to rise early enough to deliver newspapers as well as work long hours late into the night.*

Here is your chance to emphasise any special qualities

in your CV that might be overlooked, but should be good background for the job you're applying for.

> *As the fourth generation of farmers in my family, I have a keen interest in ecology and climate change.*

You should mention no more than two or three points. otherwise you risk straying into the body of your CV. Remember that space in limited.

FOURTH, FINAL PARAGRAPH

This is a brief statement that repeats your interest in the role and your belief that you're a good match for the requirements. It goes without saying that you'd be very happy to attend an interview or give more information, but it's generally accepted form to mention this.

You're looking for a formula of words that looks like this:

> *This is a role I would greatly enjoy. I believe I fit your criteria well, with extensive direct experience of the requirements. I'd be delighted to discuss the position further, but if you'd like any further details at this stage, please let me know.*

That's it. You need not "thank in anticipation"; assert that you're ideal for the role; or flatter the recruiter. A simple, confirmation that you want the job, and you're keen to meet for an interview. If there is any range of dates you cannot attend, say so here.

SIGNING OFF

The convention is to sign off with "Yours sincerely," when you address a named person, or "Yours faithfully," if the addressee is not named.

In an email you can be more informal if you prefer: "Best wishes," or simply "Regards," are both perfectly acceptable to most recipients.

4 – A WORD ABOUT YOUR LANGUAGE

Your cover letter (as will your CV) will use the word "I" a lot. It's supposed to. Don't worry about it. It's not great style to begin every sentence with the same word, but if there's ever a piece of writing that permits you to use "I" over and over, it's a job application. Recruiters are looking for you to summarise why you're a good match for the vacancy – they want you to talk about yourself.

JARGON AND BUZZ WORDS

As far as possible avoid jargon. Write relaxed, natural words. They will shine through your application making you seem warm, friendly and at ease. Powerful things, words.

Many people assume recruiters want to see the latest buzz words. Some believe that using alternatives exposes them as an outsider to the holy fraternity of business insiders. Nothing could be further from the truth. Clichés set everyone's teeth on edge, and recruiters see hundreds of cover letters a day. First of all, don't title your CV "Curriculum Vitae" – people can see what it is. Just put your name.

Avoid these clichés, especially when describing yourself:

Diligent	Team player	Highly motivated
Results driven	Hard working	I'm passionate about
Dynamic	Solution oriented	Focussed
Creative	Entrepreneurial	People management skills
Project management skills	Honest	Reliable
Problem solver	Analytical	Effective
Insightful	Action oriented	Punctual

There are undoubtedly more, but these are the worst offenders. Don't just bandy these words about – explain and demonstrate how they apply to you.

For instance, instead of describing yourself as *"effective"*, explain why:

> *"I resolved 75% of queries without escalation, against a company average of 50%."*

Rather than claim you have good "people management skills", clarify:

> *"Staff turnover in my team is under 10%,*

> *compared to 33% in the company's other units."*

If you can't prove why your description is true, you shouldn't be claiming it in the first place.

A MAGIC WORD

If your cover letter is being machine-read, it will only look for matching expressions, such as the skill sets the job demands. But if your application is sifted into the "read" pile, here's a trick to lift you above the rest of the herd.

Somewhere, throw in an unexpected word or phrase; a piece of vocabulary that stands out as unusual; a single flash of colour on a dull grey background. Just the one – you don't want to come across as trying too hard or as not knowing the appropriate business language for the occasion.

Examples:

> *I saw your advertisement on gudjob.com for a pensions actuary, and I would like to <u>throw my hat in the ring</u>.*
>
> *My <u>fresh</u> approach to sales planning led to...*
>
> *I have a <u>flair</u> for...*
>
> *I have 10 years experience in the British Army's Royal Electrical and Mechanical Engineers and I <u>can bring dead vehicles back to life</u>.*

Customers say the product launches I've staged always have a certain <u>pizzazz</u>.

Just a single word can show imagination and help you stand out. It's not a must-have, but it gives your letter a certain… pizzazz.

USE THE ACTIVE VOICE:

Nothing sounds more clunky than the passive voice. It just does.

Remember the passive voice?

Active voice: *The mechanic fixed the car.*

Passive voice: *The car was fixed by the mechanic.*

The passive voice is impersonal, leaden, unfriendly language – the opposite to what you want to achieve. It can't be avoided all the time (see what I did there?), but re-read your cover letter and CV and eradicate passives as much as you can without twisting the language into a bagel.

For example:

> *I reached my full-year goals in 7 months.*
>
> Not: *My full-year goals were reached in 7 months.*

I generated 100,000 new sales leads which became 5,000 extra sales.

Not: *The 100,000 new sales leads were converted into 5,000 extra sales.*

The Advertising Society awarded my project Best In Class for Toiletries.

Not: *My project was awarded Best In Class for Toiletries by the Advertising Society*

The problem with the passive is that it makes you sound like a passenger, rather than an active participant in the endeavour you claim to have been so successful. That's not an impression you want to leave behind.

THINGS YOU DON'T NEED

Your cover letter does not need any mention of your age, national insurance number, religion, sexual preference, political allegiance or references. Nor, indeed, does your CV. You don't need to include a photo.

PROOF READ YOUR COVER LETTER AND CV

It goes without saying that an application containing

spelling and grammatical errors will give the worst impression. Check and check again. Make sure you have the recruiter's or the employer's name correct.

5 – SAMPLE COVER LETTER

The sort of layout and minimalist (that is, brief and easy to read!) content you should aim to produce is this. Note the light-touch punctuation.

John Smith
34 Davison Avenue
Oaktown
Northumberland NE42 1BH
johnxsmith@xyz.co.uk

11 May 2016

Ms Jemma Carney
HR Manager
Shackleton & Sons (Plumbing) Ltd
Shackleton House
High Street
Rothbury NE43 2JK

Re: Business and Technical Writer Ref 123 / 2016

Dear Ms Carney,

I would like to apply for the position of Business and Technical Writer, which you posted on LinkedIn.

I have a degree in Journalism, and am currently a freelance business writer, creating speeches, articles and white papers for a range of clients in manufacturing industries around the world. Over the past 10 years, I have written more than 500 technical features for publication in trade journals. I am fastidious about presenting accurate and persuasive material – I recently published a book on argument and reasoning.

I can bring considerable experience of many forms of promotional and trade writing, with a good working knowledge of editorial standards. One important personal strength is to be able to present complex topics from a simple, layman's point of view. In particular, I am able to thoroughly research technical topics and draft publishable quality information with minimal briefing.

This is a role I would greatly enjoy. I believe I fit your criteria well, with bucketfuls of direct experience in the writing you describe. I'd be very happy to discuss the position but if you'd like any further details at this stage, please let me know.

Yours sincerely,

John Smith
Freelance Business Writer

6 – ABOUT THE AUTHOR

Jack Staff is the pen name of a manager who spent a lifetime working for globally-known brands – companies, corporations, organisations and partnerships – and has seen forests perish in vain to produce cover letters and CVs. For the most part they moved from in-tray to confidential shredding with but a momentary pause before his tired, busy orbs.

As an operational manager, Jack was selected and trained by one of the largest telecoms corporations in the world to help sift through the many thousands of job applicants who applied in the "milk-round", straight from university, interview them, and approve or disapprove candidates.

In his own right, Jack has recruited, trained and managed multiple general and specialist teams in six global organisations.

Now released from the vow of corporate omertà, Jack can remove one of the most troubling elements of applying for a job – the vexed cover letter.

www.ingramcontent.com/pod-product-compliance
Lightning Source LLC
Chambersburg PA
CBHW020715180526
45163CB00008B/3095